THE GOLDEN YEARS

1951

text: David Sandison

design: Paul Kurzeja

SIENA

If any year can be said to have a character, 1951 could be described as a very mixed-up kid! Looming above the world were the double spectres of continued and spreading war in the Far East - where Communist gains in Korea, Vietnam and Tibet involved the Western allies in a series of ferocious engagements - and the development of nuclear weapons whose awesome power dwarfed anything that had gone before, but were needed, we were told, to ensure world peace!

Signs that times were getting better came in the shape of The Festival of Britain, a triumphant reaffirmation that there really was something to celebrate as Europe and the UK continued to rebuild from the still-obvious wreckage of World War II.

Notable departures included UN Commander Douglas MacArthur - fired for speaking his mind too openly one time too many - and the immortal Joe Louis, who went one fight too far with Rocky Marciano. A divided British Labour Party mourned the death of Ernie Bevin, an old street-fighter they needed more than ever as the electorate tired of post-war austerity and demanded more candy now.

Arrivals which would impact on history included the British troops who invaded Suez to grab Egypt's main asset, and the triumphant return of Winston Churchill to 10 Downing Street and the world stage. By year-end there were signs that the Korean conflict could be settled round a conference table. But trouble continued to brew in South Africa and Kenya, and Iran began flexing its well-oiled muscles.

The old order was changing, no doubt. Sadly, the new order didn't look any more organized.

BBC Cut Accents And Women

BBC radio news bulletins are to be read only by men with 'consistent' pronunciation and performance, and no women are to be heard reporting war and disaster items under changes announced in London today.

Trimming its news and continuity staff to eight from the 19 once on air, the BBC confirmed the elimination of regional accents from its national networks, the Light and Home Services. Local accents may still be heard on regional broadcasts, however. The no-women rule? 'People do not like momentous events such as war and disaster to be read by the female voice', explained a spokesman.

French Save Hanoi

A major victory for the French in Vietnam today as they repelled North Vietnamese leader Ho Chi Minh's Viet Minh guerrillas from the South Vietnamese capital Hanoi to reverse a string of defeats in Tonkin.

The Viet Minh left behind 6,000 dead and 500 prisoners as the forces of the new High Commissioner and Commander-in-Chief, General Jean de Lattre de Tassigny - known as 'King Jean' because of his aristocratic and elegant manner - over-ran their positions around Hanoi. The victory was observed by General Brink, head of the US Indo-China mission, who reported to President Truman before a Washington meeting at month-end with Rene Pleven, the French Prime Minister.

Nevada Desert Rocked By Nuclear Test

WIND RUSHED THROUGH the streets of Las Vegas and the residents of Boulder City reported rooms lit up by a flash of light as the US Atomic Energy Commission exploded the second of two nuclear bombs in as many days in the Nevada desert. Las Vegas lay 45 miles from the boundary of the test grounds, while Boulder City was 100 miles from the explosion site.

Keen to allay the natural fears of people in the region, the Atomic Energy Commission issued a statement saying patrols had found 'no indication of any radiological hazards' after the tests. But it had asked for all civil aircraft flights within a 150-mile radius of the site to be grounded.

JANUARY 26

UN Halts North Korean Offensive

AFTER ALMOST THREE WEEKS of setbacks following a joint Chinese-North Korean onslaught launched over the 38th Parallel border between North and South Korea on New Year's Day, UN forces finally halted the enemy on a broad front south of the South Korean city of Osan.

During the fighting, which saw the South Korean capital Seoul fall to the Communists for the second time in the seven month war, the UN's American, British and Australian forces also lost control of the strategically-important town of Wonju before bombarding the port of Inchon to halt North Korea's progress.

Rumours that UN Commander General Douglas MacArthur planned to pull his troops out of Korea and fight a direct war with China were officially denied mid-month when the US Air Force and Army Chiefs of Staff, Generals Vandenberg and Collins, flew to MacArthur's headquarters in Tokyo with a message from President Harry Truman: there would be no pull-out.

While admitting the US had not been able to send in as many reinforcements as it wanted, Collins told a press conference at the 8th Army HQ that they would shortly be sending the first of many recruits mobilized under a selective training scheme.

Although not short of reinforcements, the Chinese are known to be experiencing growing communications and supply problems as they advance. Bombed incessantly and subject to repeated land attacks, they are being forced to back off to positions nearer Seoul.

JANUARY 8

Unity For Germany?

Chances of the reunification of Germany seemed to improve today when West German Chancellor Adenauer accepted an East German invitation to commence talks.

The country has been divided since the end of WWII in 1945, when USSR leaders stamped their authority on all territory to the east of their final positions and installed a regime sympathetic to communist dogma.

JANUARY 27

Less Meat For Brits

Already rationed by pricing restrictions to no more than four ounces of beef steak or five ounces of imported lamb chops a week, slim post-war Brits were told today that a breakdown in talks between Britain and Argentina meant a further trimming of their already-meagre allowance.

While the country experiences a growing meat black market and butchers are compensated for their losses, it's reckoned it would take three whole ration books to buy a pound of steak – or 13 for the unimaginable luxury of a leg of lamb.

JANUARY 15

War Bill Mounts

The true cost of the Korean War was revealed in Washington and London this month, adding fire to the arguments of anti-war lobbyists in Britain and the US.

On January 15, President Truman asked Congress for $60 billion to prepare US forces for action, while on January 29 Prime Minister Clement Attlee announced his intention to spend £4,700 million over the next three years and recall 255,000 reservists for active service.

FEB

No Love Lost As Sugar Ray Massacres La Motta

THE PLACE: CHICAGO. You know the date, so it's not hard to figure why sports writers called the bloody battle for the world middleweight title between 'Sugar' Ray Robinson and 'The Bronx Bull', Jake La Motta, 'The St. Valentine's Day Massacre'.

The two had met five times before, once in 1942 and twice in both 1943 and 1945. La Motta had won only once, at their second meeting in February '43. But that defeat - the only one he'd experienced in his first 133 fights - was one Robinson was still determined to revenge.

Back then they'd been welterweights, but La Motta had moved up a division to become world champ. Robinson had run out of opponents worthy of his strength and skill, so he set his sights on La Motta once more.

For 12 rounds Robinson piled on relentless pressure to wear La Motta out. One of the boxing world's greatest rivalries ended in the 13th when the referee stepped in to end the massacre and award Robinson the title by a technical knock-out.

FEBRUARY 26

US Presidents Limited To Two Terms

Future American presidents are to be limited to a maximum two-term, eight years in office after the 36 states needed to ratify an Amendment to the US Constitution today voted through a 22nd Amendment designed to curb presidential power.

Opponents argued the Amendment would result in lame-duck second terms for those re-elected. The only past president who would have been restricted by this change was Franklin Roosevelt. Elected four times, he died after serving 12 years in The White House.

Shah's $1.5 Million Show-Off

With his repressive authoritarian regime under attack from Islamic fundamentalists and the majority of his subjects living in poverty, the Shah of Persia displayed an arrogant lack of tact this month when he showed off the wedding dress made for his new wife, Soraya Esfandayiari. Encrusted with $1.5 million worth of diamonds, the dress characterized the gulf which now exists between the Shah and the people of Iran.

FEBRUARY 9

Garbo Becomes A US Citizen

In New York today, the increasingly-reclusive Swedish-born movie actress Greta Garbo raised her right hand and, by swearing to defend the US Constitution, became an American citizen. Garbo, whose aloof sensuality created a storm when she first arrived in Hollywood in the late 1920s, made her last screen appearance in 1941.

5: Francois Mitterand, a young French junior minister, officiated at the opening of the new Ivory Coast port of Abidjan.

8: Cecil Day-Lewis elected to the Professor of Poetry post at Oxford University.

8: HM King George VI received a 10 per cent rise in pay, the first in his 14-year reign.

16: One of Britain's leading department store chains, The John Lewis Partnership, announced the appointment of a woman managing director, Miss M.J. Ahern.

21: A new transAtlantic record crossing made by the Canberra, Britain's first jet bomber - England to Canada in 4 hours 40 minutes. (see picture over page)

FEBRUARY 1

More UK Price Hikes

As Britain sloshed
through the wettest
February on record since
1870, two price increases
were announced to add
to the mid-winter
gloom.

On February 1, coal
and coke prices were put
up as demand outstripped
supply, even with
increased imports of
foreign fuels.

The cost of keeping out
the cold rose on
February 16 when the
government added 1/8d
(almost 10p) to the price
of a standard bottle of
whisky. Those fancying a
nip would now have to
pay £1 15/- (£1.75p)
for a bottle of Scotland's
best-loved export.

British built Canberra bomber set a new transAtlantic crossing record of 4hrs 40mins

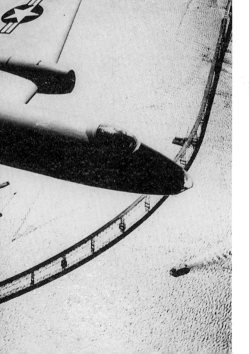

Clearer Signal For Posh BBC

Last month's decision by the BBC to have an 8-man, no-woman newsreader team for its Light and Home Service networks was followed on February 1 by the publication of the names of those who will share duties. It includes wartime stalwart Alvar Liddell and a young Robert Dougall.

Their acceptably-posh tones may come over even clearer soon. On February 6, the BBC said its Very High Frequency (VHF) test transmissions had been 'very successful'.

FEBRUARY 17

UN Push To Recapture Seoul

KOREA WAS THE SETTING for three major offensives today as South Korean, US and British troops battled their way towards Seoul and the 38th Parallel on two coastal fronts while Communist forces in the centre of South Korea beat back a UN attack.

The successful Allied advances saw South Korean infantry drive up the east coast highway to the border supported by a naval bombardment, while the western coast attack by US and British troops resulted in the recapture of the strategic port of Inchon and the shelling of communist positions in Seoul.

While the central North Korean–Chinese thrust is similar to their successful advance last November, this time Allied forces are making ground on the flanks to open the possibility of a pincer movement.

Meanwhile, UN detachments set in a 25-mile arc south of Seoul are being held up by stiff communist resistance and the natural obstacle posed by a frozen Han River.

MAR

Oxford Sunk In Boat Race

To the delight of Cambridge supporters and the amusement of non-partisan observers, the annual University Boat Race was called off today when the Oxford University boat sank mid-competition. Two days later the Oxford crew's spirits were sunk when Cambridge beat them by 12 lengths in the re-run.

MARCH 7

Iran Explodes As Premier Killed

Last month's ostentatious marriage of the Shah appears to have been the final excuse for Iran's Muslim fundamentalists. The country collapsed into turmoil today when the Prime Minister, General Ali Razmara, was shot dead by a member of an extremist sect, The Crusaders of Islam.

The assassin, a 26 year old carpenter, said his actions were forced by growing foreign influence in Iran. His victim, while responsible for a campaign against government corruption, had just signed a new deal with the Anglo-Iranian Oil Company to boost oil production and income. Within a week troops and tanks patrolled the streets of Teheran after riots and an unsuccessful attempt to kill Minister of Education Dr. Zangeneh. In what is seen as a

government bid to pacify fundamentalists, the lower house of assembly, The Majlis, unanimously voted to nationalize the oil industry. While the upper house approved the nationalization bill on March 14, only 27 of 60 Senators were present. Iran also invited foreign oil experts to run the industry when the British - developing Iranian oilfields since 1909 - finally leave.

MacArthur Threatens To Invade China

GENERAL DOUGLAS MACARTHUR, America's pro-Consul in Japan and commander of UN forces in Korea, today stepped out of line to widen the gulf between himself and President Truman when he demanded permission to carry the war to China by attacking Manchuria.

Describing the Chinese region as a 'privileged sanctuary', the General argued that existing restrictions on his freedom to hit the vast stocks of Chinese arms, troops and supplies in Manchuria should be removed.

While MacArthur's demands have the growing support of Republicans in Washington, they come at an especially bad time for the President. He and UN leaders are working on a political settlement of the war, their hands paradoxically strengthened by MacArthur-led successes in South Korea, including the recapture of Seoul.

MacArthur's threats to North Korea and Chinese territory are therefore viewed as extremely unhelpful, to say the least.

MARCH 2

UK Government Defeated

With its slender majority of six over all opposition parties since the general election of 1950, Britain's Labour government suffered defeat by four votes in a debate on the shortage of raw materials. So began a traumatic month for Prime Minister Clement Attlee.

On March 9 he shuffled his pack to appoint Herbert Morrison his new Foreign Secretary in place of Ernest Bevin who moved to become Lord Privy Seal.

ARRIVALS

Born this month:
1: Mike Read, UK disc-jockey, TV presenter, biographer and songwriter
4: Kenny Dalglish, Scottish soccer player, manager Blackburn Rovers FC; Chris Rea, UK rock guitarist, songwriter
16: Kate Nelligan, UK stage and film actress; Ray Benson, US country singer, musician (Asleep At The Wheel)
17: Scott Gorham, UK rock musician (Thin Lizzy)
20: Madan Lal, Indian cricketer; Jimmy Vaughan, US rock/blues musician (Fabulous Thunderbirds)
24: Peter Powell, UK disc-jockey
25: Maizie Williams, US pop singer (Boney M)

DEPARTURES

Died this month:
6: Ivor Novello, UK actor, playwright, songwriter (see main story)
22: Willem Mengelberg, Dutch classical conductor

4: The first-ever Asian Games opened in New Delhi, India

16: Fourteen people died when an express coach hit the mouth of a tunnel near the Yorkshire town of Doncaster

19: West Germany, France, Italy and the Benelux signed a treaty to initiate a European Coal and Steel Community

20: Britain's Field Marshal Montgomery is appointed America's General Dwight D. Eisenhower's deputy at Supreme Headquarters, Allied Powers Europe (SHAPE)

31: New Delhi: Indian Prime Minister Pandit Nehru offered his help to try bring a truce in the Korean War

MARCH 9

New Separation Rules For Divorce

A glimmer of light for those in Britain trying for years to have separation included in the grounds for divorce. Members of Parliament today approved a government Bill to add separation to adultery and cruelty as a way out of dead marriages.

Only one snag – the minimum qualifying period has been set at 'not less than seven years'.

A second snag would crop up in April with far bigger problems to face, the government withdrew the Bill

MARCH 12

Hiss Loses Appeal

In Washington, the Supreme Court rejected the appeal of alleged spy Alger Hiss, sentenced to a five-year prison sentence in January 1950 for perjury.

The jury at his first trial for espionage had failed to reach a verdict and no evidence of his spying for Russia was presented during a second hearing which outside observers criticized as a witch-hunt.

MARCH 6

Ivor Novello Bows Out

Ivor Novello, the Welsh-born matinée idol who became a prolific playwright and composer, died today aged 58.

Novello, whose real name was David Ivor Davies, specialized in performing and writing musical comedies although he was also author of a number of dramas, some of which were filmed in the 1920s and '30s.

His most famous song was the patriotic Keep The Home Fires Burning, and his legacy lives on in the prestigious annual Ivor Novello Awards for songwriters.

New Spy Fever As Rosenbergs Convicted

AS WESTERN COUNTRIES experienced the Red Menace first-hand in Korea and rumour-mills still churned over the espionage convictions of Alger Hiss and Klaus Fuchs in 1950, New Yorkers Julius and Ethel Rosenberg couldn't have faced spying charges in a more hostile climate.

Their three week trial ended today with 32 year old Julius - an Army Signal Corps engineer - and his 35 year old wife pronounced guilty of passing US atomic secrets to the Russians at the end of WWII.

Key witnesses in the couple's trial were Ethel's brother, David Greenglass, who admitted complicity in their treason, and close friend Harry Gold, already serving 30 years in prison.

The Rosenbergs, who protested their innocence throughout, were sentenced to death by Judge Irving R. Kaufman on April 5. After numerous appeals through the US legal system, including their argument that a death sentence was applicable only in time of war and the USSR had then been a US ally, they were both sent to the electric chair on June 19, 1953.

Humphrey Bogart in The African Queen

AMERICAN IN PARIS SWEEPS AWARDS

Gene Kelly had to be content with a consolation Honorary Oscar as *An American In Paris,* the hit musical in which he'd sung and danced, dominated the ceremony with a handful of awards, including the most-prized Best Picture. In fact, the multi-talented Kelly didn't even appear in the final short list for the Best Actor award. That went to Humphrey Bogart for his *tour de force* appearance in John Huston's *The African Queen,* beating off the challenges of Marlon Brando (for *A Streetcar Named Desire*), Montgomery Clift (*A Place In The Sun*), Arthur Kennedy (*Bright Victory*) and Frederic March (*Death Of A Salesman*).

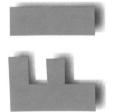

American In Paris director Vincente Minnelli also failed to win his category, and George Stevens was voted Best Director for *A Place In The Sun,* also defeating John Huston, Elia Kazan (*A Streetcar Named Desire*) and William Wyler (*Detective Story*) in the process.

Katharine Hepburn, Bogart's widely-tipped co-star in *African Queen* also lost out in the Best Actress stakes. That was won by Vivien Leigh for *Streetcar,* so eclipsing Shelley Winters (*A Place In The Sun*), Eleanor Parker (*Detective Story*) and Jane Wyman (*The Blue Veil*). *A Streetcar Named Desire* also proved the ideal vehicle for Karl Malden and Kim Hunter as they won the Supporting Actor and Actress awards.

But it was the year of *An American In Paris* in most other respects. Other Oscar winners connected with it included Alan Jay Lerner (for Best Story and Screenplay), Johnny Green and Saul Chaplin (Best Score), Alfred Gilks and John Alton (Color Cinematography), Cedric Gibbons and Preston Ames (Color Art Direction) and Orry-Kelly, Walter Plunkett and Irene Sharaff (Color Costume Design).

As Gene Kelly walked up to accept his Honorary Oscar to honour his 'versatility as a singer, dancer and director', he must have had the quiet satisfaction of knowing that his most recent enterprise - the self-directed *Singin' In The Rain* - was busy proving itself the international box-office smash of 1951.

Gene Kelly in the year's box-office hit Singin' in the Rain

APRIL

75 Die As UK Sub Sinks

All 75 crewmen aboard the 1,600 ton British submarine HMS Affray died tonight when it failed to re-surface after diving off the English south coast.

An emergency search by naval craft equipped with the latest echo-sounding gear initially found only the remains of a number of wartime German U-boats, and it would not be until June 14 that the Affray was finally located in 258 feet of water.

A survey of the craft led to the Admiralty banning the use of 'Snort' breathing tubes on British subs when it was discovered that the Affray's had developed a fatal fault.

APRIL 14

Labour Reels As Bevin Dies And Bevan Quits

BRITAIN'S LABOUR GOVERNMENT was hit by a double whammy this month with the sudden death of party firebrand and wartime Minister of Labour Ernest Bevin, and the stormy resignation of Aneurin (Nye) Bevan, its dynamic new Minister of Labour of only three months.

Although Ernest Bevin's death on April 14 at the age of 70 was not entirely unexpected - he'd suffered declining health for some time, hence his sideways shuffle on his birthday in March - Labour had lost a powerful figurehead and Prime Minister Attlee a valuable ally.

A mix of ruthless, humane and shrewd, Bevin had risen from childhood poverty to become Britain's most powerful trade union leader. He masterminded the mobilization of 22 million troops and workers as a member of Churchill's wartime coalition cabinet before helping plan and manage Labour's massive victory in the 1945 general election.

The April 22 resignation of Aneurin Bevan, a fervent left-winger adamantly opposed to the current level of defense spending, would prove the opening salvo in a vicious war between Labour Party factions.

Joined in his walk-out a day later by two disciples, Board of Trade President Harold Wilson and junior War Office minister John Freeman, Bevan quit rather than agree with Chancellor of the Exchequer Hugh Gaitskell's plan to impose Health Service charges on previously-free false teeth and spectacles.

Carnage At Grand National

Those who say The Grand National - arguably the world's most famous and formidable steeplechase event, which pits the cream of international riders and horses against 30 fences and four and a half miles - is too dangerous and should be banned, had their prejudices confirmed today. Only three of the 36 horses which started the National at Liverpool's Aintree Racecourse managed to finish. While most suffered no or slight injuries (except to pride), there were some equine fatalities in a race won by Nickel Coin.

APRIL 4

Suez Troop Pull-Out Promise

Following five months of secret talks in London and Cairo, the British government today approved, in principle, to Egyptian demands for the withdrawal of British troops from the Suez Canal area.

The call for UK military to leave the strategically-important Canal Zone first came in November, when King Farouk used the annual state opening of the Egyptian Parliament to insist on evacuation, a revision of the 1936 treaty between Britain and Egypt, and the unity of Egypt and Sudan.

APRIL 12

Britons Killed In Iran Oil Riots

Two women and a child were among eight Britons killed in the oilfields of Bandur Mashur and Abadan today as rioting spread among striking workers breaking into the installations of the newly-nationalized (see March) Anglo-Iranian Oil Company.

At Abadan, which boasts the world's largest oil refinery and is the heart of Iran's industrial base, martial law was declared and police opened fire on marauding crowds led by fundamentalist agitators demanding the seizure of all foreign assets.

The Abadan complex was closed down on April 15.

APRIL 11

Police Recover Stolen Stone

A 107-day nationwide hunt for The Stone of Scone, the ceremonial sandstone slab stolen by independence-seeking Scottish Nationalists from beneath the Coronation Chair at Westminster Abbey in December, was today recovered by police in Arbroath, Scotland.

The 458-lb stone, which historians say was taken from Scone in Scotland by King Edward I in 1296 and placed in Westminster Abbey to signify the English crown's domination of the Scots, was the subject of a huge petition demanding Scottish independence.

Those responsible had promised King George that their unusual hostage - known as The Coronation Stone in England - would not be damaged. Experts confirmed that it was indeed intact on recovery.

Truman Fires MacArthur - Ridgway Takes Over

A STUNNED AMERICA WOKE this morning to learn that President Harry Truman had stripped the highly-popular General Douglas MacArthur of all his duties, including that of Supreme Commander, United Nations Forces in Korea.

The controversial move was announced at one o'clock in the morning, after which The White House released a series of documents to show that MacArthur had repeatedly ignored warnings from the President against making political statements. His replacement is to be Lt. General Matthew Ridgway.

Explaining his decision in a networked broadcast, President Truman said US policy in the Far East was designed to stop the conflict spreading. 'So far we have prevented World War Three', he said.

'A number of events have made it evident that General MacArthur did not agree with that policy', the President added. 'I have therefore considered it essential to relieve him so there would be no doubt or confusion as to the real purpose of our policy'.

True to form, an unrepentant MacArthur had his say. Interviewed on March 19, he defended his bellicose stance, describing Truman's Korean policy as 'blind to reality'.

APRIL

MAY 17

British And Anzacs Kill 400

Four hundred Chinese troops were killed today as British, Australian and New Zealand forces repelled a mass attack on their lines south of Chunchon. Attacked by artillery and tanks, the Chinese showed none of the suicidal bravery which marked other recent advances, most notably the action against the Gloucestershire Regiment at the Imjin River which saw an outnumbered British force holding out.

MAY 23

Generals Attack MacArthur

The row over President Truman's dismissal of General MacArthur rumbled on as two of America's top generals criticized their former comrade at a Senate committee inquiring into his departure.
 Both General Omar Bradley, Chairman of the Joint Chiefs of Staff, and General George C. Marshall, Secretary of Defense, backed Truman's decision.
 General Bradley said MacArthur's plan to extend the war into China would have led to ' the wrong war, at the wrong place, at the wrong time and with the wrong enemy '.

MAY 4

Festival Lets GlimpseThe

IT COST OVER £8 MILLION - more than critics said a still-impoverished country could afford. It included a new, ultra-modern, stylish concert and classical music venue, The Festival Hall. It featured a host of new inventions and designs under a vast construction known as The Dome of Discovery. Its 27-acre site on the south bank of the Thames transformed a derelict bomb site into a kaleidoscope of light as a funfair, riverside walkways and a fun railway designed by cartoonist Roland Emett vied for the attention of awe-struck visitors.

Officially opened today by King George VI and Queen Elizabeth, The Festival of Britain allowed a nation still beset by post-war austerity, fuel shortages, food rationing and international strife to let its hair down and catch a glimpse of how the future might look.

Described by Festival director Sir Gerald Barry as a triumph of 'fun, fantasy and colour', the Dome of Discovery was created by a design team led by architect Hugh Casson to provide a spacious centrepiece full of gentle curved surfaces.

Dominating the site, apparently suspended in mid-air, the neon-lit futuristic shape of The Skylon loomed like a giant aluminium exclamation mark.

Planned to coincide with the 100th anniversary of Prince Albert's Great Exhibition in 1851, the Festival of Britain would end in September, leaving only The Festival Hall as a lasting memory of a brief but glorious celebration.

Britain
Future

ARRIVALS

Born this month:

1: Gordon Greenidge, West Indian cricketer

3: Christopher Cross, US pop singer

4: Chris Frantz, US rock musician (Talking Heads, Tom Tom Club)

11: Mike Sleman, UK rugby player

13: Selena Scott, UK TV presenter; Paul Thompson, UK rock musician (Roxy Music)

16: Pierce Brosnan, Irish film actor

18: Rodger Davis, Australian golfer

23: Anatoly Karpov, Russian world champion chess master

27: John Conteh, UK boxer, former WBC light-heavyweight champion

DEPARTURES
Died this month:
27: Field Marshall Sir Thomas Blamey, Australian soldier
29: Fanny Brice (Fanny Broach), US comedienne
30: Herman Broch, Australian poet and novelist

MAY 12

Pacific Test For H-Bomb

THE TINY PACIFIC CORAL ISLAND of Eniwetok was the scene of the first hydrogen bomb test carried out today by the US Atomic Commission and Department of Defense. Although an official statement was light on details, the Commission said the test had exceeded expectations.

The hydrogen bomb, which will be hundreds of times more powerful than the atomic bombs which destroyed Hiroshima and Nagasaki in 1945, worked by fusing the nuclei of hydrogen atoms at incredibly high temperatures. It required an atom bomb to create those temperatures and act as a trigger.

While the successful test indicated a strong US lead in the nuclear field, it also signalled a new and more hectic round in the international arms race as Russian scientists set about creating their own destructive devices.

24

MAY 27

Tibet Offered Religion Deal

The tiny mountain Buddhist state of Tibet, invaded by the Chinese last year, was today promised religious freedom only on condition that its mineral wealth can be exploited and it severs 'all pro-imperialist ties'.

The one-sided 17-point pact was agreed by a delegation sent to Peking by the Dalai Lama, Tibet's exiled 16 year old spiritual and temporal leader, who also surrendered control over his country's army and foreign policies.

South Africa Ends 'Coloured' Vote

An historic watershed today in South Africa as the Afrikaner Nationalist government voted to remove so-called Coloured (mixed race) voters from the electoral register, a franchise they've held since the Cape became self-governing under the British in the last century.

Dr. Theophilus Donges, Minister of The Interior, said the action was needed to avoid 'the collapse of white civilisation in the whole of Africa'. The predominantly English-speaking United Party rejected the move during a heated debate, but lost the deciding vote 74-64. With millions of black South Africans unable to vote, the country became a white enclave.

JUNE

International Hunt For Burgess And MacLean

TWO WEEKS AFTER they mysteriously vanished from London, British diplomats Guy Burgess and Donald MacLean officially became the subject of an international hunt today when the British government asked police in Britain, France, Austria and Germany to help locate and apprehend them.

The security implications of their disappearance were serious. Both had served in sensitive Washington posts - MacLean (38) was First Secretary in the British Embassy before returning to London to become head of the American Department of the Foreign Office, while Burgess (40) was Second Secretary in Washington for eight months before having a nervous breakdown. While official sources in London were still being coy about a possible double defection to the Soviet Union and would only confirm that both had been suspended for being absent without leave, US papers openly voiced suspicion and official concern with Soviet links.

The mystery deepened on May 8 when the diplomats cabled London to say they were taking 'a long Mediterranean holiday'. Three days later, government minister Herbert Morrison admitted that security aspects of the case were 'under investigation' with a special watch being made on the border between the British and Soviet zones in Austria.

Russians Propose Korean Ceasefire

The United Nations was sent into a flurry of diplomatic activity today by a surprise call for a Korean war ceasefire from the Soviet Union's senior delegate, Jacob Malik.

Immediate Western reaction to the Soviet proposal was positive, though cautious. The year-long war, which began as a local territorial dispute but became an international conflict, was believed to have been encouraged by Russian leader Josef Stalin's supply of arms to North Korean leader Kim Il Sung. On June 30, UN chief General Matthew Ridgway confirmed that he was ready to negotiate a ceasefire with Communist leaders.

JUNE 7

Princess Stands In For Sick King

PRINCESS ELIZABETH, the 25 year old heir to the English throne, was the surprise stand-in when she took the salute at today's Trooping the Colour ceremony in London.

The central role at this annual parade of Guards regimental colours, or ceremonial flags, is traditionally taken by the reigning monarch. The absence of King George through illness was to be the first indication that his health was beginning to deteriorate.

JUNE 13

De Valéra Returns As Irish PM

Eamonn de Valéra returned to power today as prime minister of Eire following the election defeat of a coalition government led by John A Costello and the collapse of the Republican Party's vote. De Valéra, whose election campaign was greatly aided by Catholic Church opposition to the coalition's health policies, was bitterly opposed to their acceptance of the British Ireland Act, which recognized Ulster's status, and pledged to increase state benefits and tackle rising inflation.

Hot Wheels In Action

Excitement in the world of motor racing this month: on June 17, Italy's Giuseppe Farina won the Belgian Grand Prix at Spa for Alfa-Romeo, edging compatriots Alberto Ascari and Luigi Villoresi's Ferraris into second and third places. Eventual world champion, the Argentinian Juan Manuel Fangio, turned in a record-breaking 120.51 mph lap.
On June 24, Peter Walker drove his Jaguar to victory in the Le Mans 24-hour marathon, the first Briton to win for 16 years.

UK Rejects Iran Oil Plan

Three weeks after President Truman warned Britain and Iran that their dispute over the nationalization of Iranian oilfields was potentially explosive, the 8,000-ton cruiser *Mauritius* lay at anchor in the Shattel-Arab waterway today, ready to move up to the Abadan oil refinery and evacuate British oil workers.

The 2,500 British employees of the Anglo-Iranian Oil Company have told the fiercely nationalist government of Dr. Mohammed Mossadegh they will not work in a nationalized corporation, eight days after the government broke off talks and two days after Dr. Mossadegh introduced a bill imposing heavy penalties on anyone trying to sabotage the oil industry.

JUNE

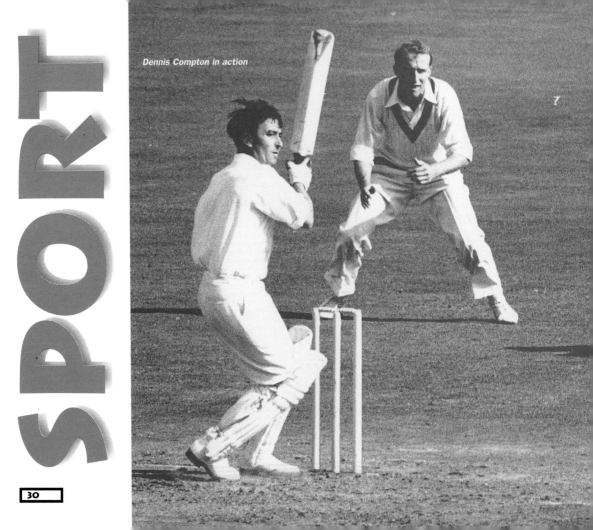

Dennis Compton in action

SPORT

MIXED YEAR FOR ENGLISH CRICKET

ngland's selectors had their fair share of headaches in 1951 as they struggled to pick a team capable not only of winning a Test series, but proving consistent in all departments. The year started miserably as England were thrashed 4-1 by Australia in their winter test series, and could only scrape a 1-1 result against the unfancied New Zealand.

England began no better in their series at home against South Africa's tourists, losing the first Test by 71 runs when SA bowlers Mann (with a 4-24 tally) and Rowan (5-68) tied down England's batsmen after Simpson and Compton had both made centuries to give the home side a decent start.

Blushes were spared by series end, however, as England emerged victorious with a 3-1-1 record.

ENGLISH SOCCER TEAM RECOVER LOST DIGNITY

Still reeling from their ignominious first-round exit from the 1950 World Cup in Brazil when defeat by a US team of semi-pros and amateurs ended the progress of their internationally-renowned squad, the English soccer team spent the 1951 season rebuilding their reputations.

All in all, they succeeded pretty well. They enjoyed wins over Argentina at Wembley (2-1), Portugal at Goodison Park (5-2) and managed draws with France and Austria (both 2-2).

The only real hiccup in England's comeback to respectability came in the annual battle with eternal enemies Scotland at Wembley, losing 3-2 to a Scottish team which also notched up wins against Denmark (3-1), France (1-0) and Belgium (5-0) before losing to Austria (0-4) and Wales (0-1).

Tottenham emerged as English League champions, with Manchester United runners-up, while Newcastle United beat Blackpool 2-1 to win the FA Cup. In Scotland, Hibernian ended the First Division championship 10 points clear of second-place Rangers, but were beaten 3-0 by Motherwell in the League Cup final. Celtic stopped Motherwell's hopes of a double by beating them 1-0 in the Scottish FA Cup.

RAMS BASH BROWNS

Last year's American Football champions, The Cleveland Browns, had the tables turned on them in this year's championship game when the LA Rams - the team they'd beaten 30-28 with a last-minute Lou Groza field goal in their first season in the NFL - emerged as 24-17 victors.

The Rams' heroes at the Memorial Coliseum were quarterback Norm Van Brocklin and receivers Tom Fears and Elroy 'Crazy Legs' Hirsch. During the season Hirsch had shattered Don Hutson's receiving record with 1495 yards and 17 touchdowns, and he combined with Fears for 212 yards on eight receptions to dominate stats which included sacks of the Browns' Otto Graham for 47 yards in losses.

It was a fourth quarter 73 yard throw by Van Brocklin to Fears which gave the Rams their winning touchdown and ended a record-breaking season for Van Brocklin, who'd entered the history books when he passed for 554 yards during his team's win over the New York Yanks.

Norm Van Brocklin
- a record breaking season

JULY

Turpin Steals Sugar Ray's Crown

IN ONE OF THE BIGGEST UPSETS in modern boxing history, British middleweight Randolph Turpin tonight comprehensively beat the legendary Sugar Ray Robinson at London's Earl's Court stadium to become the first UK fighter to hold the world title since Bob Fitzsimmons in 1891.

The 23 year old Turpin entered the ring a clearly unfancied challenger. Since taking Jake La Motta's title six months earlier, Robinson had defeated eight opponents, six of them European. The best odds being given for a Turpin points win were 20-1 against, despite a creditable 41-victory record and being the British and European champ.

Disorientating Robinson with a short left hook in the second round, Turpin kept up relentless pressure to win nine of the 15 rounds and leave Robinson requiring 14 stitches over a badly-damaged eye.

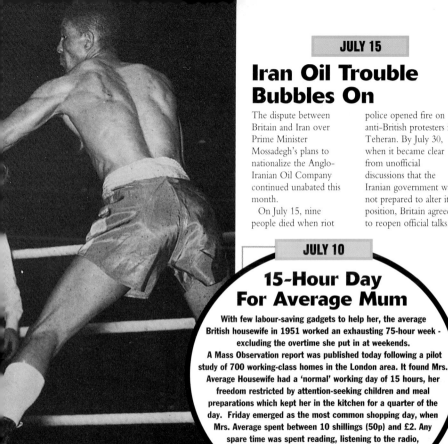

Iran Oil Trouble Bubbles On

The dispute between Britain and Iran over Prime Minister Mossadegh's plans to nationalize the Anglo-Iranian Oil Company continued unabated this month.

On July 15, nine people died when riot police opened fire on anti-British protesters in Teheran. By July 30, when it became clear from unofficial discussions that the Iranian government was not prepared to alter its position, Britain agreed to reopen official talks.

15-Hour Day For Average Mum

With few labour-saving gadgets to help her, the average British housewife in 1951 worked an exhausting 75-hour week - excluding the overtime she put in at weekends.

A Mass Observation report was published today following a pilot study of 700 working-class homes in the London area. It found Mrs. Average Housewife had a 'normal' working day of 15 hours, her freedom restricted by attention-seeking children and meal preparations which kept her in the kitchen for a quarter of the day. Friday emerged as the most common shopping day, when Mrs. Average spent between 10 shillings (50p) and £2. Any spare time was spent reading, listening to the radio, watching TV or going to the cinema.

NEWS IN BRIEF

1: Argentina's Juan Fangio won the 374-mile French Grand Prix (the world's longest motor race) at Rheims

7: At Wimbledon, American Richard Savitt became Men's Champion when he beat Australia's Ken McGregor 6-4,6-4, 6-4. The Ladies final was an all-US affair with D. Hart beating S. Fry 6-1, 6-0.

13: The Queen laid the foundation stone of the new National Theatre in London

20: The maiden flight of Britain's new Hawker Hunter jet

26: British golfer Max Faulkner won £1,700 when he became British Open champion at Portrush, Co. Antrim, Northern Ireland

JULY 20

Assassin Slays King of Jordan

A STATE OF EMERGENCY was declared in Jordan today following the fatal shooting of King Abdullah outside the Mosque of Omar, one of Islam's holiest shrines. The assassin, a local tailor called Mustafa Shakir who belonged to an anti-Abdullah organization, The Sanctuary of Struggle, was killed by the King's bodyguards.

Reports from the mosque described Shakir springing from behind a gate and shooting King Abdullah in the back from close range before guards could stop him.

Abdullah's younger son Emir Naif was proclaimed Regent - the rightful heir, Emir Talal, was being treated for a nervous breakdown in Beirut.

The dead sovereign had ruled for 30 years, first as Emir of TransJordan and later as King of Jordan. He was viewed by many Palestinians as a traitor for diverting his Arab Legion to occupy and annex East Jerusalem, territory they claimed as part of their homeland, during the Arab-Israeli war.

JULY 11

British Population Up

Proof that Britain is busy rebuilding itself after the trauma and losses of WWII came today with the first publication of results from the national census held in 1950. The population of England and Wales has grown by 3.8 million to 43,744,924 in the 20 years since the last pre-war survey.

Korean Ceasefire Talks Open

JULY 26

The first substantive talks on a Korean War ceasefire were held today in a tea-house when delegations led by Admiral Joy of the US Navy and General Nam II of the North Korean army met for the first time.

The talks were held in a neutral zone established in the town of Kaesong after UN Commander General Matthew Ridgway agreed to a meeting on July 2. Initial discussions dealt with arrangements for a demarcation line and demilitarized zone to separate the two sides.

Truce supervision and prisoner of war exchanges were also on the agenda.

Observers reported the atmosphere as 'cautious and mutually-distrustful', and predicted that talks would be drawn-out and acrimonious while people continued to be killed.

Vichy Traitor Petain Dies

A hero during WWI and leader of the Vichy government which collaborated with the Nazis to govern France during WWII, Marshal Philippe Petain died today, unmourned by millions who survived the German occupation. He was 95.

Petain, who was arrested in 1945 while attempting to flee into neutral Switzerland, had been sentenced to death when tried and found guilty of treason.

His sentence was commuted by General De Gaulle because of his age. One of his principal collaborators, Pierre Laval, who had twice acted as the Vichy government head, was executed in October 1945, aged 62.

UK Oil Workers Leave Iran As Talks Fail

AFTER THREE WEEKS of fruitless talks to reach a compromise in the Iranian oil nationalization dispute, it seems that Britain's 41-year interest in the Persian oil industry is over. The Anglo-Iranian Oil Company today ordered all British, Pakistani and Indian workers to leave.

Although there's virtually no chance of a last-minute change of heart by Iranian Prime Minister Mossadegh - who recently demanded and won a vote of confidence for his stance in Iran's parliament, the Majlis - staff at the Abadan refinery will stay for the time being to prove Britain is not deserting Iran.

The deal which Lord Privy Seal Richard Stokes, head of the British mission, tried to sell to Dr. Mossadegh would have seen a joint Anglo-Iranian agency operating the oilfields on behalf of a National Iranian Oil Corporation, and UK firms allowed to sell the oil internationally.

Some Majlis deputies have publicly claimed their government-supporting 'yes' vote was dictated by threats from extremist Islamic fundamentalists.

New Music Maker Arrives

It was 12 inches in diameter, made of a black-coloured flexible petroleum-based material called vinyl, revolved at a very slow 33 revs per minute, and could contain an entire symphony on its two sides. The first long-playing record was released in Europe today by the West German company Deutsche Grammophon, changing the way we listened to our favourite music forever.

Austin Increase A40 Price

Unwelcome news for British motorists, especially those who planned to buy a new A40 (below) - one of the UK's best-selling family saloons Austin, the company who make the A40, today announced they were raising its price by £31 to £685.

Anti-US Demo In East Berlin

In a triumphant show of government organizing skills, more than a million young East Germans massed in East Berlin today to stage a 'spontaneous' protest against Western powers in general, and US policies in particular.

The demonstration came coincidentally only 11 days after President Truman ended all trade tariff privileges still enjoyed by Communist countries - East Germany included.

NEWS IN BRIEF

10: Cuba and Britain signed a trade pact which should improve UK sugar shortages

15: Architect Basil Spence won a competition to design a new cathedral in Coventry to replace the one destroyed by German bombs

18: In Washington, official figures showed the average US income in 1950 was $1,436 (about £472)
Jamaica: 132 died when the island was hit by a hurricane

25: Belgrade – Emmanuel MacDonald Bailey set a new world 100 metre record of 10.2 seconds

30: Wales – 75 Welsh nationalists protested against the War Office's purchase of land in the Trawsfynydd area

ARRIVALS

Born this month:
2: Andrew Gold, US singer/songwriter; Steve Hillage, UK rock musician
3: John Graham, US pop/soul musician (Earth Wind & Fire)
4: Peter Squires, English rugby player
13: Dan Fogelberg, US singer/songwriter
19: John Deacon, UK rock musician (Queen)

DEPARTURES

Died this month:
14: William Randolph Hearst, US press magnate *(see main story)*
15: Artur Schnabel, Austrian concert pianist
21: Constant Lambert, English composer and music critic

AUGUST 29

Cautious Optimism In Korean Peace Talks

A GLIMPSE OF LIGHT at the end of the tunnel in the Korean War peace talks in Kaesong today as a United Nations statement described a 'more temperate' approach by the North Korean's delegation leader General Nam Il.

UN press officer Brig-General Nuckols told world pressmen that the Communists appeared to have relaxed their dogmatic position. He said delegates had found enough common ground to begin serious discussions on a ceasefire.

Proof of North Korea's change of heart first came on August 5 when the Communists apologized for an incident when some of their troops entered the truce zone. The greatest threat to UN forces has come from freak storms. A number of men with the 1st Commonwealth Division died when their positions were hit by lightning and flash floods.

AUGUST 24

Mau Mau Influence Spreads

Kenyan police today publicly linked a series of burglaries in the white suburbs of the capital Nairobi to the secret political society called Mau Mau, and admitted a growth in its influence among black Africans seeking independence from Britain.

Authorities have been aware of the sinister Mau Mau's existence for about a year and only know that oaths to drive the white man from Kenya are sworn by Kikuyu tribe recruits attending secret meetings in the forest outside Nairobi.

A large number of suspected Mau Mau members have been arrested in recent weeks, though the names of their leaders are not yet known for certain.

'Citizen' Hearst Dies

William Randolph Hearst, the American press baron whose extraordinary life inspired Orson Welles' 1941 film classic *Citizen Kane,* died today in Beverley Hills. He was 88.

Unwilling to join his wealthy father's business, a young Hearst asked for a present of the staid *San Francisco Examiner* newspaper. Transforming it via a scandal-led circulation war, Hearst went on to build a nationwide chain of 18 papers and nine magazines, many specializing in lurid sex and crime stories.

Hearst's personal life was equally exotic. He funded a number of films by his long-time mistress, Marion Davies, and built two immense castles (San Simeon Castle pictured) in California, both stuffed with priceless *objets d'art.*

AUG

BIG HITS FOR BIG-VOICED MARIO

The pop chart appearances of Luciano Pavarotti in the early 90s were remarkable, certainly. But they were nothing compared with the international impact enjoyed in 1951 by Mario Lanza, the 30 year old American matinee idol operatic tenor.

Signed to a 10 year recording contract by RCA Victor in 1945 after completing US military duties, the Philadelphia-born Lanza (real name Alfred Cocozza, pictured right) had quickly established himself on the American classical concert stage, including a 1948 New Orleans operatic debut in *Madam Butterfly*.

Spotted by MGM scouts, Lanza made his first film appearance in the 1949 movie *That Midnight Kiss,* but it was the 1950 *The Toast Of New Orleans* which helped break him through to pop stardom.

Released as a single in late 1950, *Be My Love* benefited from its inclusion in that film. By March 1951 it had become America's No.1 seller, crossing over the Atlantic to lodge at the top of the British best-sellers for a staggering six months between April and September.

Between July and October it was joined at No.2 in

the UK lists by Lanza's *Loveliest Night Of The Year,* which had given him his second US chart-topper in September - just as his third film *The Great Caruso* became a huge hit worldwide.

Although he would enjoy further success with songs like *Because* and *Because You're Mine* in the years before he died of a heart attack in Rome aged only 38, Lanza knew that 1951 had been very special.

LES AND MARY MAKE IT BIG IN BRITAIN

American pop duo Les Paul and Mary Ford - he a nimble-fingered guitarist and arranger who baffled record-buyers with his multi-tracked brilliance, she a pleasant jazz-tinged singer - made their international breakthrough in 1951 with four huge hits.

Two of those - *Tennessee Waltz* and *Mocking Bird Hill* - made the top of the British lists. The first, which was Britain's most popular record between January and May, had been America's No.1 in December 1950. In April it was joined at the top in the UK by *Mocking Bird Hill*. Their second US smash of 1951 (in March they'd scored with *How High The Moon*), the song was also a big hit for Patti Page.

Before year-end they'd notched up two more big US successes. In July they scored with *The World Is Waiting For The Sunrise,* and returned in December with *Just One More Chance.*

JIMMY BEATS NAT IN 'TOO YOUNG' BATTLE

British cover versions of American hits often fared well in the fifties as local artists were able to marshall support not only from their fans, but also from radio bosses who'd often give the UK alternative more airtime on key request shows.

However, the American originals inevitably fared

better in sales terms. No matter how popular a British performer may be, the Yanks made far better records - and they did have the allure of stardom.

The second half of this year produced a remarkable tussle for British chart supremacy with the song *Too Young.* Originally a major hit for Nat 'King' Cole in the US, it had been quickly covered by the aptly-named British crooner Jimmy Young. Both versions raced up the UK chart to lodge at No.1 and No.2 for all of August to December - the Brit for once emerging winner.

Nat Cole had the last laugh, however. By mid-October his version of *Too Young* was joined in the Top 3 by *Because of You,* a record which finally toppled Jimmy Young's cover and stayed the British No.1 until February 1952.

BREAKTHROUGH FOR BENNETT

One of the most dramatic new arrivals of 1951 came with the emergence of a New York-based one-time member of Bob Hope's road show, the velvet-voiced Tony Bennett.

Born Anthony Benedetto in Queens, Bennett had been signed to Columbia Records by Mitch Miller in 1950. His first single, *Because Of You* also became his first No.1 million-seller in September 1951 - a feat he repeated in November when the double A-sided *Be My Love/Cold, Cold Heart* produced a smash hit in the latter.

By year-end the 25 year old newcomer was celebrating two more hits - *Blue Velvet* and *Solitaire* - to confirm his genuine star status.

Jimmy Young won the battle of 'Too Young'

SEPTEMBER 12

Robinson Regains Turpin's Title

When Sugar Ray Robinson lost his world middleweight championship to Randolph Turpin in July, it was widely believed he neither took the Briton's challenge seriously, nor was in good enough shape.

The American hero didn't make the same mistakes tonight when the two met again in New York. While Turpin looked to be on the way to a successful defense of his title, a heavy right from Robinson in the tenth round put the Englishman down. The referee stepped in soon after to stop the fight and declare Robinson champion again.

NOVEMBER 11

Czechs Take Fast Track West

The stream of people fleeing Communist-dominated eastern Europe hit new dramatic heights today when 25 refugees stole a train and raced through Czechoslovakian border posts to reach West Germany. On board what press soon dubbed *The Freedom Express* were engineer Frazek Jarda, his wife and two children. He told how friends had switched points to put their train on a freight track and cut brake lines to ensure it couldn't be stopped. 'We did it because it was no longer bearable to live in an East European state', he told reporters.

SEPTEMBER 23

Major Lung Operation For King George

A HUGE CROWD GATHERED anxiously outside the gates of Buckingham Palace in London this afternoon, awaiting official word of the condition of King George, who underwent two-hour surgery to remove his left lung yesterday.

The bulletin, signed by the King's eight doctors, was finally posted in a picture frame by a palace official who carried it to the main gate accompanied by two policemen. Newsmen from around the world pressed forward to photograph the inch and a half high black crayoned letters announcing the King's condition was as satisfactory as could be expected.

Doctors had diagnosed a lung disease on September 8, but news of this was kept quiet while treatment options were reviewed and the eventual decision to operate was taken.

While Prime Minister Clement Attlee, who'd called an October general election only four days earlier, cut short a brief holiday in North Berwick to return to London, a private service for the King's recovery was held at the chapel of Lambeth Palace, London, by the Archbishop of Canterbury, Dr. Geoffrey Fisher.

Little Mo Youngest-Ever US Champ

Maureen Connolly, the 16 year old world tennis circuit's brightest new star already nicknamed 'Little Mo', became the youngest-ever winner of a Grand Slam event today when she won the US Championship to begin a glittering career which would include Wimbledon titles in 1952, '53 and '54.

SEPTEMBER 8

Russia Slams Japan Peace Treaty

NEVER ONE TO MISS the chance to accuse America of warmongering, Soviet Foreign Minister Andrei Gromyko seized on part of the peace treaty Japan signed today with 48 other nations to put an official end to World War II - a pact allowing the US to station military forces on Japanese soil.

Although the peace treaty, which comes six years after the actual end of hostilities, means Japan loses most of her pre-war empire and is barred from ever re-arming, Gromyko said Japan's punishment was 'too light'.

He also described the Japanese-US pact as proof of American 'preparation for a new war', even though the US has maintained two troop divisions in Japan for some time.

Gromyko made no reference to a Washington announcement made on September 3 that the USSR had exploded its second atomic bomb in a secret test.

SEPTEMBER 27

Germany To Compensate Jews

In an historic and emotional session, delegates to the Bundestag – Germany's national assembly in Bonn – today voted unanimously to make full restitution for 'unspeakable crimes' against the Jews during the Hitler years. Discussions are already under way to determine the extent of compensation to be paid to survivors of the concentration camps, in which around six million are thought to have died, their relatives and the families whose property was seized by the state as Jewish people's rights were withdrawn and the Nazis' Final Solution began.

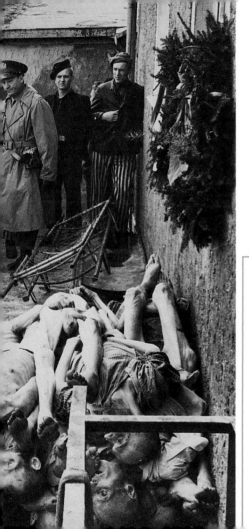

Labour In-Fighting Gives Churchill Hope

Winston Churchill's hopes of winning the General Election called by Labour Prime Minister Clement Attlee for October 25 got a boost today as the so-called Bevan Group of left-wingers led by former Minister of Labour Aneurin Bevan launched an astonishing 'own-goal' attack on their own side. They published a tract vilifying Chancellor of the Exchequer Hugh Gaitskell (already described publicly by Bevan as 'a dessicated calculating machine') whose budget introduction of prescription charges for dentures and spectacles had caused Bevan's resignation in April, and condemned the attitudes of leading trade union bosses.

Suez Issue Hots Up

Warning signs that Britain's Middle East problems are not confined to the Iranian oil nationalization dispute, which saw the UK appealing for UN intervention on September 28 when the latest round of Teheran talks reached an inevitable stalemate this month. Relationships with Egypt reached a new low on September 10 when British properties and businesses were the target of nationwide riots organized in support of King Farouk's decision to rescind the 1936 Anglo-Egyptian alliance and demand withdrawal of UK forces based in the Suez Canal zone.

The British government has steadfastly rejected Farouk's proposals to create a potentially explosive situation.

OCTOBER 17

Porsche Return Germany To Export Market

Germany's mighty car industry returned to the international arena for the first time since the end of the war when a sleek Porsche, capable of hitting 90 mph on UK roads still unfettered by rural speed limits, was the hit of this year's British Motor Show in London.

While motor experts lavished their praise on the streamlined Porsche's looks and performance, its manufacturers bent backwards to stress the car's safety features and stability, even when that near-ton was reached.

Brits Seize Suez Zone In Dawn Raid

A FLURRY OF NEGOTIATIONS between London and Cairo ended this morning with a surprise British military raid to successfully win control of all key points on the Suez Canal. There were no serious casualties for the forces of General Erskine, but two Egyptians were killed and five wounded as their positions were over-run.

The attack came five days after Britain offered to quit Suez if Egypt signed a new five-nation defense pact which would include Egypt, France, Turkey, the United States and the UK. Egypt's rejection on October 15 stung Britain into action.

Erskine's force, including crack paratroops, landed in Egypt on October 19, but their dawn strike took Egyptian commanders completely by surprise. Two days later, more British troops were en route to Egypt, with four warships docked in Port Said. On October 22 Britain halted all arm exports to its former ally.

Political Snakes And Ladders

Any month with a General Election is likely to deliver a few shifts in fortune, for better or worse. October 1951 was no exception as a number of British politicians discovered:

2: Labour's stalwart left-winger Manny Shinwell fell in the pre-election shuffle of his party's national executive committee. His place was taken by the more-moderate Barbara Castle.

25: The Conservatives' youngest candidate was 26 year old Margaret Roberts, a former research chemist. Although she failed to win the Kent seat of Dartford, Miss Roberts would return in 1959, by then the wife of wealthy businessman Dennis Thatcher, to win a place in the House of Commons.

30: Winners of the three key posts in Churchill's new cabinet: RA ('Rab') Butler as Chancellor of the Exchequer, Anthony Eden as Foreign Secretary and David Maxwell-Fyfe as Home Secretary.

OCTOBER 26

Churchill Back At Number Ten

STUNG AND HURT by the electorate's rejection of him in 1945 when he assumed Britain's voters would naturally keep their wartime leader as the nation's first post-war Prime Minister, Winston Churchill returned to power today as his Conservative Party won a narrow victory over Clement Attlee's divided Labour.

Now aged 77, Churchill left Buckingham Palace after accepting his commission from King George - apparently recovering well from his major surgery last month - to say he relished the chance to revitalize Britain's fortunes by freeing the country from Labour's socialist ideals and alleged mismanagement.

The final score in yesterday's election gave the Tories 321 seats, Labour 295, Liberals 6 and others 3. Commentators viewed the collapse of the Liberal vote - they fielded candidates in only one constituency in six and attracted two million fewer votes than in 1950's stalemate election - as a vital factor in Churchill's victory.

Recognizing this, the new Prime Minister offered Liberal leader Clement Davies representation in his cabinet, an offer Davies refused.

Even as votes were being counted, a bitter and public Labour post mortem saw furious left-wingers accuse their leader of losing the election by betraying socialism. While they fought it out, the Conservatives began to honour campaign promises to create a 'strong and free' Britain.

Marciano Stops Louis In Eight

A living legend was humbled in New York tonight when former world heavyweight champion Joe Louis fought one fight too many and was beaten into retirement by a tough 28 year old fast-riser, Rocky Marciano.

Broke, badly-advised and not discouraged by his unsuccessful bid to regain his crown from Ezzard Charles in 1950, The Brown Bomber attempted one more come-back in a long and distinguished career which had seen him beaten only twice before - by Charles and, in 1936, by Max Schmeling.

With title-fight recognition riding on the fight, Marciano showed scant respect for Louis and when he smashed the veteran through the ropes in the eighth round, the ref stepped in to end the carnage.

OCTOBER 31

Britain Falls To The Spell Of The Box

Only two years since the BBC expanded its television reach by opening regional transmitters, firstly in the Midlands and this year in the Manchester area, figures published today suggest Britain can't get enough of the magic box in the corner of the sitting room.

According to TV manufacturers, although the total number of British homes with televisions was only 344,000 in 1950, demand in newly-reached areas is such that they will be making 250,000 this year alone.

While the BBC began the world's first regular TV service in 1936, there were only 100,000 viewers 10 years later, all in the London area. When a Scottish transmitter is opened in 1952, four-fifths of the UK population will be able to pick it up.

OCT

OCTOBER 6
WILLIAM KELLOGG

Although rivals have come and gone - and some have done well enough to survive as runners-up in certain countries - breakfast cereal packs with the distinctive Kellogg symbol would probably match Coca-Cola in an international logo-recognition contest.

The man responsible for such an astonishing achievement, William (Will) Kellogg, died today at the age of 90 knowing that his legacy consisted not only of one of the world's most successful business empires, but also a charitable foundation bearing his name and dedicated to improving the welfare of children everywhere his company's wide range of products were sold.

Will Kellogg was the first to acknowledge that the family's fortunes would not have existed without his brother's inspiration and perserverance. The head of a sanitorium in Battle Creek, Iowa, it was Dr. J.H. Kellogg's idea to create a palatable corn-derived food he believed would benefit his patients.

The result was so good the brothers began to market corn flakes and in 1906 Will bought his brother out to form the Kellogg Toasted Corn Flakes Company. Early competition came from Post Toasties, a company founded by a former Battle Creek patient, but the combination of Will Kellogg's business acumen, his tireless development of new cereal products and his acquisition of other food companies reinforced the Kellogg dominance.

By 1930 the multi-millionaire Will was able to create the WK Kellogg Foundation and eventually pass the day-to-day running of the family empire to the next generation, secure in the knowledge that his family's name had won a place in history.

JULY 31:
EVONNE GOOLAGONG

An inspiration to a generation of teenaged Australian girl tennis players in the seventies, and an even greater inspiration to native Australians still treated very much as second-rate citizens, the skills, grace and power of part-Aborigine Evonne Goolagong also won her countless fans around the world as she competed for top titles in major tournaments.

Overshadowed during her initial rise by fellow Aussie Margaret Court, Evonne achieved international star status at Wimbledon in 1971 when she beat the highly-fancied Billie Jean King in the semis before defeating Court to take the title in straight sets.

The following year saw King stop Evonne from regaining her title, and it would be another three years before she reached the Wimbledon final again, when she (a recently married and re-named Evonne Cawley) once again lost to King.

While she continued to prove a leading attraction and consistent winner on the pro tennis circuit, the Wimbledon jinx continued in 1975 when a young Chris Evert beat her in the final. In 1980 Evonne had her revenge - and her second Wimbledon title - when she defeated the now-married Chris Lloyd.

OCTOBER 2:
STING

Born this day in Wallsend, near Newcastle-upon-Tyne, this phenomenally-successful rock musician/writer/actor/conservation activist began life as Gordon Sumner. His stage name was given him by a fellow musician when he appeared in a yellow and black-hooped bee-like T-shirt.

Qualifying as a primary school teacher, Sting moonlighted with various jazz and rock bands before moving to London in 1976 and joining The Police as bassist, lead singer and group songwriter in 1977.

During the next eight years The Police were one of the world's biggest-selling rock acts, although Sting had made his intentions of pursuing his own solo goals from the beginning. In 1979 he made his movie acting debut as the super-mod Ace in *Quadrophenia,* since when he has starred (with mixed critical results) in a number of other films. In 1985, with The Police effectively disbanded, Sting began his solo career proper, choosing mainly to develop a jazz-biased style. A vocal contributor to the 1984 famine fund-raising *Do They Know It's Christmas?* single, Sting's humanitarian concerns have included work for Amnesty International, Greenpeace and his funding of the campaign to help the Kayapo tribe's fight to save their Brazilian rainforest homeland.

Never one to go with the flow, Sting continues to make challenging music and to challenge the political *status quo.*

WENT

NOVEMBER 11

Evita III, Peron Wins

An up-and-down day for the Peron family in Argentina. Although his wife Eva (right) - the former actress and singer known to her devoted followers as 'Evita' and universally recognized as the dominant and domineering member of the team - was only slowly recovering from serious ovarian cancer surgery, Juan Peron (far right) was re-elected President of Argentina today. His victory came despite increasing unrest at widespread graft and nepotism within his administration, which was founded with the stated intention of aiding Argentina's impoverished peasants.

NOVEMBER 7

Conservatives Take And Give

While they were naturally occupied by events in Egypt and Korea, Britain's new Conservative government was also finding ways to deliver on election promises to revitalize an economy they say Labour wound down.

Chancellor of the Exchequer Rab Butler opened his account on November 7 with a rise in bank lending rates - from 2.0 percent to a relatively-large 2.5 percent.

On November 29 there was good news for Britain's farmers, however. The government announced plans to boost farming subsidies by £26 million ($78m) to aid much-needed domestic production of staple foods.

British Evacuate Families From Egypt

AN INCREASINGLY UNCOMFORTABLE and dangerous time for the 2,000 British women and children trapped in Egypt since the UK take-over of the Suez Zone ended today as a mass evacuation of dependants began from Ismailia. Before being shipped out, they'd been trapped in their homes as riots and a shooting war broke out between local police and occupying British forces.

Five Britons and nine Egyptians were killed as local police responded to orders from Cairo to fire on military vehicles before British Commander General Erskine persuaded the Egyptian governor of the Canal Zone to disarm them.

The government in Cairo declared a state of emergency on November 6 after the British carried out the biggest troop airlift since the war. Minister of the Interior, Serag-El-Din Pasha, described the invasion as 'wanton, barbaric agression against innocent civilians and police'.

Jeering crowds at Ismailia saw the evacuation as Egypt's first victory in the struggle to get the British out. Five days later they took control of the town and by month-end Britain had agreed to withdraw from three others if the Egyptians promised to subdue terrorism.

Malayan Troubles Increase

Tension continued to build in Malaya, where communist guerrilla forces have stepped up pressure following their assassination of British High Commissioner Sir Henry Gurney last month. They have hit the country's vital rubber industry hardest and 16 major plantations were today reported to have suspended work following terrorist threats to native employees.

NOVEMBER 28

All Quiet On The Korean Front

SILENCE FELL ON front-line trenches in Korea today following a ceasefire agreement which established a truce along the pre-war North-South frontier, the 38th Parallel.

Although no official orders for a cessation of hostilities were given, officers on both sides had been told not to carry out offensive actions while a full armistice was agreed by negotiators in Keosong. The successful conclusion of their efforts merely formalized an existing state of affairs.

It's not the end of haggling, however. There still remains the obstacle of prisoner of war repatriation to be overcome, with many thousands being held behind both sides of the ceasefire line.

Truman Backs Ike

Having secretly decided not to seek re-election as President, Harry Truman (far left) and Democratic Party bosses have begun to sound out potential candidates they hope will succeed him to The White House after the 1952 elections.

The President made it clear today which of the most likely front-runners he'd be prepared to sponsor - WWII hero, D-Day invasion mastermind and current Supreme Allied Commander in Europe, General Dwight D Eisenhower (left).

NOVEMBER 24

Austin And Morris Merge To Create Giant

The world's fourth biggest motor manufacturing company - after the American 'Big Three' of Chrysler, General Motors and Ford - was created today when Britain's two leading car firms, Austin and Morris, agreed merger terms.

It is the second time the two have tried to unite. In 1948 they attempted standardizing components and sharing information, but this arrangement failed.

Assuming the deal goes through when a necessary 90 per cent of ordinary share-holders accept a swap of each company's holdings, the first Chairman of Austin-Rover will be Lord Nuffield. Deputy Chairman and Managing Director will be Leonard Lord, Austin's current Chief Executive.

NOV

Missing PoWs Storm Sours Korean Peace Talks

PROGRESS IN THE KOREAN ceasefire talks was halted today when the UN delegation accused the Communists of failing to account for more than 50,000 Allied prisoners of war - a charge rebutted with the reply that most of the supposedly-missing had been released at the war front while the rest had died of sickness or been killed in Allied bombing raids.

With a four-day deadline set for all outstanding differences to be settled if the existing truce line ceasefire is to hold, a UN spokesman said the Communists had 'to all intents and purposes rejected the Allied proposal' to an immediate exchange of wounded and sick PoWs.

There is Allied anger at the huge difference between original figures of prisoners the Communists said they were holding - more than 63,000 - and their revised total of only 11,000. On December 21, Supreme Commander General Matthew Ridgway called for the Red Cross to be allowed to visit communist PoW camps.

Hopes of a peaceful Christmas appear to be fading. Distrust of the Communists' intentions led Major-General Cassels, Commander of the Commonwealth Division, to add a warning to his Christmas message: 'The enemy may well think that he may catch us unprepared...I know I can rely on you to prove him wrong'.

DECEMBER 24

Libya Declares Independence

The former Italian colony of Libya was today proclaimed an independent state, 13 months after a UN resolution began the ball rolling for the North African nation.

King Idris el Senussi announced Libya's new status as the Kingdom of Libya in a broadcast from his capital, Benghazi, during which he paid tribute to all who'd taken part in the struggle for freedom. Among the first countries to recognize Libya's independence was Italy, with whom there had been lengthy negotiations to safeguard Italian business interests and the safety of 40,000 Italian nationals living or working in Libya.

DECEMBER 3

East Germany Rejects Olympic Invitation

With the 1952 Olympic Games due to take place in Helsinki, Finland, the organizers were able to strike at least one name off their list of potential contestant countries today when East Germany delivered a firm 'Nein' to their invitation. Their reason? The Olympic committee have also invited West Germany to participate, and the East German regime refuses to recognize their rival neighbours' right to a legitimate presence on any world stage.

NEWS IN BRIEF

1: England: Critical acclaim for the premiere of composer Benjamin Britten's opera *Billy Budd*.

4: More than 20 were killed when a bus careered into a company of Marine cadets in Chatham, Kent

6: Tehran, Iran – Riots saw bloody clashes between 10,000 police and students

11: Vietnam – French troops under siege in Tonkin as Viet Minh guerrillas launched a huge offensive

29: Washington – US Atomic Energy Commission announced it could produce electric power for industry and homes from nuclear energy

Naval Books Top Best-Sellers

A year-end review of book sales in Britain and America reveals that the biggest-sellers of 1951 have both been World War II naval dramas.

In the US, Herman Wouk's *The Caine Mutiny* - the story of a deranged captain whose officers take command of his ship - was the year's No.1. When filmed in 1954, it would produce the last great performance of Humphrey Bogart's career. Britain's big-seller, Nicholas Montsarrat's *The Cruel Sea,* would also make it to the silver screen in 1952 and give Jack Hawkins the chance to keep his upper lip stiff as a British naval commander battling German U-boats on Atlantic convoy runs.

Nobel Winners Named

Nobel Prizes were awarded in Stockholm and Oslo today, with the coveted Peace Prize being given to the French socialist leader and pre-war trade unionist Leon Jouhaux. The Literature crown was given to Swedish writer Per Lagerkvist.

The Physics Prize was shared by British scientist Sir John Cockroft and Ireland's Ernest Walton, while two Americans - Edwin McMillan and Glenn Seaborg - won the Chemistry Prize. South African physician-scientist Max Theiler was awarded the Medicine Prize.

Brits Under Fire In Suez Riots

THIRTY-THREE PEOPLE - including three British and six Mauritian soldiers - were killed and more than 60 injured, as troops of the Royal Sussex Regiment came under fire from a group of 40 Egyptians in the second day of riots near the town of Suez.

The situation has been confused by an agreement reached a week ago between the British Commander, General Erskine, and the Egyptian government. This effectively handed back maintenance of civil law and order to re-armed Egyptian police, who are clearly siding with civilian guerrillas.

The guerrillas are also getting support from the Egyptian government which a few days ago gave medals and promotion to Ismailia policemen who fired on British troops in last month's riots.

Local newspapers today filled their pages with news of the Suez fighting which resulted in a British move to seal off the town by stopping trains and other traffic, except those carrying essential supplies, from entering or leaving.

The press have accused British forces of firing on a hospital and using artillery in built-up areas, accusations which have been strongly denied by UK spokesmen.

Leigh And Olivier Hottest Ticket

The hottest ticket in London's theatreland this December was for the two-play production starring Britain's matinee idols Vivien Leigh and husband Laurence Olivier in the George Bernard Shaw and Shakespeare versions of the Cleopatra legend at The St. James's Theatre.

Leigh, whose appearance in the smash movie *A Streetcar Named Desire* (pictured below with Marlon Brando) has made her a hot tip for the Best Actress Oscar in next year's Academy Awards (a prize she would win), played Cleopatra in both plays, while Olivier alternated as Caesar or Antony. Not everyone was entirely swept away by Leigh's acting. Waspish critic Kenneth Tynan was content with her sex-kitten Cleo in the Shaw play, but wrote that she played the Shakespeare queen of the Nile 'with her little finger crooked'.

Unlike most Western horoscope systems which group astrological signs into month-long periods based on the influence of 12 constellations, the Chinese believe that those born in the same year of their calendar share common qualities, traits and weaknesses with one of 12 animals - Rat, Ox, Tiger, Rabbit, Dragon, Snake, Horse, Sheep, Monkey, Rooster, Dog or Pig.

They also allocate the general attributes of five natural elements - Earth, Fire, Metal, Water, Wood - and an overall positive or negative aspect to each sign to summarize its qualities.

If you were born between February 17, 1950 and February 5, 1951, you are a Tiger. As this book is devoted to the events of 1951, let's take a look at the sign which governs those born between February 6 that year and January 26, 1952 - The Year of The Rabbit:

THE RABBIT
(FEB 6, 1951 - JAN 26, 1952)
ELEMENT: METAL   ASPECT: ▬

Rabbits are peace-loving creatures who hate anything to do with violence, brutality and war, will avoid physical conflict throughout their lives and are committed pacifists. These traits make them good negotiators and communicators of ideas, always compromising to a conclusion which will satisfy all concerned.

Contrary to what one might think, Rabbits do not lack courage. If all peaceable solutions fail, they will fight bravely for their principles.

Rabbits are wise and intuitive creatures, and often streetwise when it comes to world affairs. They see things coming and are always prepared to handle situations by putting themselves in other people's shoes - talents which ensure that Rabbits enjoy financial stability and security throughout their lives.

Rabbits possess a natural mothering instinct and are ideally suited to all domestic activities. Home is the centre of their universe and everything revolves around making it secure. They have an eye for beauty, are often stylish with good taste and artistic potential, but are better recognized for their appreciation which often leads to Rabbits becoming great collectors.

Sensitivity and artistic appreciation often combine to make Rabbits outstanding musicians.

While some Rabbits are described as cold individuals who dislike physical contact, this coolness is essentially a means of masking their deeply sensitive nature - but that sensitivity can also account for Rabbits' notorious moodiness and a tendency to swing from elation to depression at the drop of a hat.

Method, order and routine are important to the Rabbit's well-being - they need a carefully-planned existence.

This does not mean Rabbits are boring, however. They do appreciate sociability and can be friendly and chatty. They also possess the most cultivated social graces and can always be distinguished by their sense of refinement and cultured views. Physically and intellectually elegant, Rabbits will always stand out in a crowd.

FAMOUS RABBITS

Fidel Castro
President of Cuba

John Cleese
Actor, writer

David Frost
TV personality/ interviewer

James Galway
Classical flautist

Ali McGraw
Film actress

Bob Geldof
Musician(founder of The Boomtown Rats) human rights activist/organiser of Live Aid

Henry Miller
Author - *Tropic of Cancer*, etc

Orson Welles
Film actor/director/ writer